W9-BHB-392

Rookie
Read-About® Science

It Could Still
Be Endangered

By Allan Fowler

Consultants

Linda Cornwell, Coordinator of School Quality
and Professional Improvement
Indiana State Teachers Association

Janann V. Jenner, Ph.D.

Children's Press®
A Division of Grolier Publishing
New York   London   Hong Kong   Sydney
Danbury, Connecticut

Visit Children's Press® on the Internet at:
http://publishing.grolier.com

Designer: Herman Adler Design Group
Photo Researcher: Caroline Anderson

The photo on the cover shows a Bengal tiger.

Library of Congress Cataloging-in-Publication Data

Fowler, Allan.
    It could still be endangered / by Allan Fowler.
        p. cm. — (Rookie read-about science)
    Includes index.
    Summary: Presents many animals that are extinct or endangered, such
as the bald eagle, passenger pigeon, and American bison, tells what has
caused their numbers to dwindle, and suggests how they might be saved.
    ISBN 0-516-21208-7 (lib. bdg.)   0-516-27088-5 (pbk.)
    1. Endangered species—Juvenile literature. [1. Endangered species.]
I. Title. II. Series.
QL83.F68   2000
333.95'42—dc21   98-22036
                                                        CIP
                                                        AC

GROLIER
PUBLISHING

At one time, millions of passenger pigeons lived on Earth. Today there are none. People killed them all for food.

Passenger pigeon

Many of the animals that now live on Earth may also disappear forever.

Bald eagle

A mother manatee with two calves

This means they are endangered. Bald eagles, manatees, and Bengal tigers are all endangered.

Mountain gorilla

African elephant

An animal could be as strong as a mountain gorilla or as big as an elephant and still be endangered.

An animal could be as playful as a sea otter or as gentle as a giant panda and still be endangered.

Sea otter

Giant panda

A scientist watches young sea turtles as they head for
the ocean.

All over the world people are working to make sure that no more animals are lost forever.

People help sea turtles by collecting their eggs, so they will hatch on a safe beach.

People help California condors by catching them and raising chicks in zoos.

In 1987, only seven were alive in the wild. Today there are more than one hundred.

California condor

13

Leopard

California condor

Leopard

American alligator

People help leopards and alligators by stopping hunters from killing them for their fur or skin.

People have also helped
gray wolves and black-
footed ferrets.

Gray wolf

Black-footed ferret

18

The best way to save animals is to save the places they live.

People must stop polluting the lakes, rivers, and oceans where fish live.

People must not build farms and towns on the grasslands where bison live.

Bison

Poison–dart frog

People must not cut down
the rain forests where
poison-dart frogs live.

People must not drain the wetlands where whooping cranes live.

Whooping crane

This cheetah lives in Masai Mara National Park in Kenya, a country in Africa.

26

Many endangered animals
now live in national parks.

Animals are safe in national
parks because people cannot
change the land or hunt the
animals there.

Let's hope that someday there will be no more endangered animals.

Bighorn rams are endangered animals.

Words You Know

bison

black-footed ferret

California condor

leopard

30

manatees

mountain gorilla

passenger pigeon

sea otter

whooping crane

Index

About the Author

Allan Fowler is a freelance writer with a background in advertising. Born in New York, he now lives in Chicago and enjoys traveling.

Photo Credits

©: Animals Animals: 10 (Doug Wechsler); BBC Natural History Unit: 25, 31 bottom right (Thomas D. Mangelsen); Dembinsky Photo Assoc.: 21, 30 top left (Skip Moody); ENP Images: 8, 31 bottom left (Gerry Ellis), Jeff Vanuga: 17, 30 top right; Peter Arnold Inc.: 18 (IFA), 13, 30 bottom left (Ted Schiffman); Photo Researchers: 5, 31 top left (Douglas Faulkner); Tony Stone Images: cover (James Balog), 6, 31 top right (Daniel J. Cox), 29 (Darrell Gulin), 15 (David Muench), 14, 26, 30 bottom right (Manoj Shah), 7 (Robert Stahl); Visuals Unlimited: 22 (A. Kerstitch), 16 (Joe McDonald), 4 (Arthur Morris), 9 (Fritz Pölking), 3, 31 center left.